So you want to be a
Tax Agent

So you want to be a Tax Agent

Tax Agent

A survival guide to working in Public Practice

Linda McGowan

STEAM AHEAD
publishing

Steam Ahead Publishing

First Printing, 2020

Title: So you want to be a Tax Agent
Layout: Pickawoowoo Publishing Group
Printing & Distribution: Ingram (USA, UK, AUS, EUR)

STEAM AHEAD
publishing

Publisher: Steam Ahead Publishing

ISBN 978-0-6488695-3-5 (hardback)
ISBN 978-0-6488695-0-4 (paperback)
ISBN 978-0-6488695-1-1 (e-book)

NATIONAL
LIBRARY
OF AUSTRALIA

A catalogue record for this
book is available from the
National Library of Australia

CONTENTS

INTRODUCTION

Make no mistake about who is paying you. Yes, it's your employer but who pays them? The client does.

When a client walks in the door of your practice, they are bringing with them a whole lot of trust. Trust that you'll do your best by them. Trust that you'll protect their information and not lose it. Trust that you will have their back with the Tax Office, ASIC and any other regulator.

Clients won't ask about how well you did in your exam. They won't ask you whether you have enough experience to handle their tax or accounting work. You won't be asked "will you get me the best refund you can?"

If you are sitting with a client and providing any advice or support, the client will assume that you are technically competent and able to help them.

Many years ago I attended hear Dr Padi Lund speak at a professional development day. Dr Lund was a dentist in Queensland but the topic he spoke about was relevant to all service providers. The message he delivered has stayed with me ever since.

He talked about the importance of Critical Non Essentials. These are the little things that clients use to assess us. How can a client without an accounting or tax background work out if we are technically proficient? They can't. They have no idea what to ask or how to test our technical training.

But they can judge us on criteria gained from their own life experience and instincts. For example, it's not essential to being a tax agent or an accountant that your office is welcoming and tidy. However, put yourself in their shoes and think about those first couple of minutes when they come in.

Would you go to a doctor where entering you heard staff talking about other patients, the office was untidy or dirty and the doctor came out not knowing your name or why you were there?

This is an example of a "critical non-essential".

Managing a client relationship is an ongoing process. It starts with the getting those critical non essentials right, then it is all about communication.

This book has all the things I have learned from being in practice over twenty-five years. As the world in which we deliver tax and accounting services change, people are still people and we need to communicate with our clients more than ever before.

> *Your true success in life begins only when you make the commitment to become excellent at what you do.*
> *- Brian Tracy*

Don't think that because you have prepared a tax return you have started and completed your role in managing the client relationship. The tax return is just the beginning.

Prepare for the meeting

The door opens and in walks the client. They take a seat while the receptionist organizes their beverage of choice.

What do you do? Well, it all actually started well before the client arrived.

First, it's all about you.

Take a look at yourself. Are you ready for this appointment? Have you been to the bathroom and tidied yourself up? Do you have any food stains on your clothing?

It is really important in summer but really it's just as important all year round; is your deodorant working? Splash, not soak, some body spray or aftershave on. That office is a small room so any body odour will be off putting. The same goes for your breath. Eat a mint or brush your teeth.

If you are a smoker please wash your face and your hands before a meeting and most definitely eat a mint. This is really important if you are a heavy smoker. Don't underestimate how much non smokers hate having to sit three feet from the smell of stale cigarette smoke.

The Interview Room

It might not be your job to set the interview room up but make sure the room is ready for the appointment. Things to check:

- are the lights on?
- is the room tidy and clean?
- if you are using a computer ,is it on and is the software open and ready?
- is there paper in the printer?
- are there pens and paper for you to write on? (this is important even if you are in a "paperless" office)
- jug of water and glasses?

> *Success is no accident. It is hard work, perseverance, learning, studying, sacrifice and most of all, love of what you do are doing or learning to do.*
> *- Pele*

Remember the critical non essentials that clients judge us by? How we address each client, how we present ourselves and how we talk to them are as important as the technical work we are about to undertake for them. Be prepared for the meeting. Show the client that you are respectful of the trust they are putting in you and your firm.

Get to know the client

Now, it is all about them. A few minutes before the client walks in, make sure you remember their name. Do they go by their first name, their middle name or a nickname. This is especially relevant where you are new to the practice but the client is not. It is a clear sign that you have not done any research if you do not use the name the client prefers to be called by.

I have a client whose first and middle names are Robert Campbell but he is called Adrian by his friends and family. Imagine how he feels when he receives mail from our office address to Robert when he's been a client of the practice for twenty years.

Is the client meeting just for them or is it also about their spouse or business?

Review the last return lodged and if available, the business financials. Get an understanding of the work that is needed: do they have a rental property or investments; do they have a small business; are there lots of work related deductions?

Review last year's working papers. Is the client going to bring in software and if so, do you know how to upload the data and access it? If you don't, then find out who in the office does and make sure they are available during the time of your appointment.

Does your office have a checklist or system for gathering client data in an interview? If it does, read it and get it ready for the meeting. If there isn't a system then at a bare minimum print out a copy of the last tax return lodged as a guide for the information you should be asking the client for.

Do you have all the Tax Office reports that you need? Is there any other document or file that the client has emailed through in anticipation of this meeting? It's also important to check your practice's software for any electronic file notes.

If the client has a business find out if there are any documents that need to be signed that may have been kept aside waiting for the next meeting. An example would be unsigned minutes or an ASIC form following the change of address.

Has there been a partner or staff member managing this client in the past that you can talk to? If so, ask them for a brief rundown on the client. Remember, this meeting is all about the client so find out a little bit about them as a person.

One thing a client hates is having to go through their life history just because there has been an internal change in staff in the practice.

Demonstrate to the client that you, while new to their file, have done your homework.

But if there is really no one in the practice with knowledge of the client, then be honest. Tell the client that you haven't had a chance to catch up with whoever their last contact was but that you are looking forward to working with them now and doing what you can to help sort out their query or their tax return or whatever it is that they are there for.

The Client Interview

Greeting the client

Okay, so you know who the client is, your personal presentation is immaculate and the room is ready. As you approach the client what do you do?

Smile. As you walk towards the client, look directly at them and smile. As you get nearer hold out your hand, say hello, use their name, and introduce yourself. If you do shake their hand, please use a slightly firm grip by applying some pressure when your hand makes contact.

Think of something to say appropriate to the situation, such as:

- can I give you a hand carrying anything?
- have you been offered a coffee or tea yet?
- thanks for coming in, how are you going?

During the interview

Remember to talk to the client. They might be more nervous than you are so put them at ease. Ask them if they have any questions they would like addressed. If they do, make notes and make sure you address those questions before they leave the meeting.

If you are preparing a tax return in front of the client you should be proficient enough at using the tax software that you can enter data and make small talk at the same time. If you don't know the client, keep it fairly simple until you feel a rapport building. Try neutral questions like:

- how was your day so far?
- do you have a big day ahead?

Try to get the client to feel at ease as you start to gather their information. If you're nervous or inexperienced prepare a list of questions to bring into the meeting. It is really important that you listen to the answers provided. Active listening is a very difficult skill to master. You may need to stop the task you were doing to address properly what the client has just told you.

If the client is giving you their data on a USB, don't let them leave without making sure that the data they have brought in can be accessed and is for the period covering the work you are about to do for them. It is really easy for a client to attach an old data backup by mistake. They may only perform a backup once a year or a quarter so don't assume that the data that you are given is either readable or for the correct period.

If you are not personally uploading their data, ask the person who will be doing it to bring in some reports. A good start would be the Profit and Loss for the year to date and, if it is for a BAS, for the relevant quarter. Review the reports to see if they make sense and are consistent with the last period or year. You may need to bring the prior period information with you for comparison.

Try using two screens: one screen for the tax software and the second screen for the excel spreadsheet or working papers used to capture information. Every firm has their own system but they will be broadly similar. Look carefully at the documents provided by the client. Make sure you notice:

- the date of the receipt is in the tax year you are working on;
- the item being claimed is clearly described;
- if it is for a rental property, at which address was the item installed or the service delivered;
- the amount paid is visible.

Are the claims being made this year from the client similar to claims made in the prior years? If not, is there a reasonable explanation for the difference?

Remember, keep talking to the client.

- have they been in their job a long time?
- are they enjoying their new job?
- are they hoping to make a sea or tree change soon?

Are they any items of information that the client has forgotten? If so, make sure you clearly write down all the missing items that the client is going to follow up for you. Give your client a list of information needed or email the list after the meeting.

Missing information can be frustrating but don't forget, the client is often more nervous or distracted than you so they may not recall all they need to find and bring for you to complete their tax return.

When some information does come back it is often followed by the question "do you now have everything you need to finish my return?" Before you answer, you should ensure to check the notes you made during the meeting and that everything in the interview has been either provided or explained.

It is nearly impossible to make money on the preparation of personal tax returns when you have to go to and fro chasing more information from clients. The more times we pick up and put down a simple tax return, the more money is lost for the practice. And the client will become annoyed.

If there is any additional information to be provided following the meeting, send an email to the client:

- Thank you for coming in and it was nice to meet you;
- Just as a reminder, here are the items we still need from you.

A follow up email is also a great way for any other staff member to assist the client if you are unavailable and there is a query as to what information is required. Either print out the email or store electronically and keep with the other working papers for the client.

Diarise a follow up. If you don't hear back from the client within a week at the most (unless they have already advised that they need more time) follow them up with either a reminder email or a phone call.

Remember, if all this information chasing is for a personal tax return, time has already run out on making any money on this job.

> *Confidence comes from discipline and training.*
> *- Robert Kiyosaki*

When the meeting is over

Don't just walk back to your desk. Walk with the client to door. Thank them again for coming in. Remind them that you will wait to hear back from them if they need to provide additional information.

Open the door for them and say good-bye.

If the client has another meeting within your firm or will be held up paying an account at reception, it is really important that you still:

- thank them for coming in;
- remind them that they need to get back to you with information;
- say good-bye.

During the whole meeting process the client should feel that they have your undivided attention and that you value their custom. They should not feel that they are "just another client".

Referrals from clients are not just given because you they received a great refund. Referrals come partly because you make the client feel valued as a customer.

> *If you really want to do something, you'll find a way. If you don't you'll find an excuse.*
> *- Jim Rohn*

3

What does Selling to a client mean?

"I'm an accountant not a salesperson!"

Actually, you are both. You are a salesperson because you are convincing the client to trust your technical skills and professionalism. You had to sell yourself to your employers in order to be offered a position.

Be very clear about this issue. It is not about selling products or services that the clients do not need. (It is also important not to sell products or services that the client does not understand.)

The very act of opening a Public Practice means that the firm is selling. The doors open, the lights are on and the staff are waiting for the clients to roll in. Public Practices operate in a very crowded space and there are a lot of ways an individual or business can have a tax return prepared. What does our practice offer that is different or makes us stand out in the crowd?

One thing we sell is our knowledge and experience. Here are some examples of what I mean:

- Does the client understand the impact of not being properly insured be it in life, business, income protection;
- As someone approaches retirement age do they know the importance of pre retirement planning?
- If a client has expressed an interest in leaving their job and starting a business, do they know you can help them with start up advice which to increase their chance of succeeding?

Case study 1

> You see the same family for 10 years. During this time you know that they are struggling financially and if something happened to the main income earner it would mean financial ruin. You may have thought to yourself: they should really look at income protection and life insurance. But you never said anything as you didn't want to seem nosey or pushy.

Something does happen to the main income earner and the family sit in front of you and ask "why didn't you tell me about that?" How do you feel?

You can't force a client to do something that they don't want to do. But you can take the opportunity to have them think differently, by explaining:

- what you see as a financial risk;
- a possible solution to managing that risk.

Suppose you had suggested during any of those meetings that the client talk to an insurance agent about getting insurances that will pay off their debts or provide an income stream to help pay their bills if a life changing incident occurred. It is up to the client to then decide whether they can afford the cover needed. It is the client making an informed choice that matters.

Case study 2

You see a client who has recently turned 59 years of age. They are still working and during the interview expressed how tired they were and if only they could afford to work part time. Do you finish the return and say nothing, or do you suggest that they spend some time getting advice from a financial planner so that they are fully aware of what options are available to them?

How rewarding would that next meeting be if they had taken your advice, seen a financial planner and had worked out a way to work part time and access a small pension from their superannuation?

Learn who the referrers are for the practice.

Talk to your employer/manager and find out who the referrers are for:

- Insurance
- Financial Planning
- Mortgage Broking
- Legal advice
- Leasing

Your firm may have this in-house or they may have other businesses that they refer to. If a client is seeing a financial planner offer to hold the meeting in your offices. It is a great opportunity to offer to sit in on the meeting with the client. There are often tax issues raised which you will be able to address immediately. It is also a great way for you to gain an insight into a different professional disciplines and learn how professionals can work together.

If you cannot sit in on the meeting suggest to the client that they forward a copy of the advice to you. That way you not only learn what advice the client has been given, but you can keep a note on file for the next tax return. It is important to work co-operatively with other professionals as ultimately you are all there providing support to your client.

> *Great things in business are never done by one person. They're done by a team of people.*
> *- Steve Jobs*

Preparing a tax return for a client is a "sale" for the practice. Suggesting to a client that they seek advice on solving an issue that you have raised as a potential "risk" to the client is not only being helpful but deepening the practice's relationship with that client.

When you are referring a client to another professional advisor it is vital that you keep in mind that the client should never feel that doing business with you is contingent on their using a referral service. This is true even if the referring advisor is closely related to your employer.

If the client doesn't like the advice from a suggested referrer ask why. Give their feedback to your employer or manager as it may reflect a broader issue with that referrer. Then, if you can, suggest a second option. Reassure the client that it is important that they feel comfortable with the advisor and the advice given. You will work with whoever the client ultimately decides is their preferred choice of advisor.

4

Managing your productivity

Why is productivity so critical yet often misunderstood?

Do you have a clear understanding of what Income you are expected to generate for the firm? Is it three times your salary position or higher?

Managing your productivity is not only how you keep your job, it is also how to discuss pay increases and other opportunities. It doesn't matter whether you work in a large firm or small, the principles are the same.

It is important that you understand that you are not just "buying" yourself a job. If all you can invoice out is barely equal to your own salary package then you are not contributing to the practice overheads or making any money for your employer.

Practice overheads include:

- rent, stationery, phones, power and advertising;

- costs and maintenance of your computer system;
- software costs;
- admin staff who support the accountants;
- coffee or tea that you have during the day;
- depreciation of the desk you sit at and equipment you use;
- training.

The cost of simply opening the office each morning, before paying staff, is enormous and rising yearly. What you produce needs to pay for your share of those overheads.

Your employer has given you a job and both of you have responsibilities. Your responsibilities include covering your costs, contributing to the practice overheads and then rewarding your employer with some profit for the business risk they continuously bear.

Let's look at the four factors that are taken into account:

1. Your salary position is your cost to your employer and is your salary plus the Super Guarantee mandated employer contributions.
2. How many weeks do you work in a year?
3. How many hours per week are you expected to be chargeable?
4. What is your charge out rate to the client?

1. What is your salary position and what fees do you need to generate?

The first factor should be very easy for you to calculate. So let's say you are on a salary including super of $60,000. If your employer is expecting you to earn three times your cost, you need to earn / invoice out $180,000. This means actual invoices to clients. Not just time on a time sheet but real invoices to clients where the invoices are actually paid.

If you are working as part of a team, make sure you find out what your team's time/cost budget is. Every job will have some element of admin time and review time. For instance, the client will either drop in the year end tax work or has a meeting. Admin support logs the job in, collates tax reports or gets the job ready for an accountant in other ways. By the time an accountant looks at the work, there may be two or three hours already on the clock. You do your part of the work, it is then reviewed and, if needed, amended, then finally printed and collated for the client.

Whether you work as part of a team or are wholly responsible for the process of preparing a client's work, if a mistake is made and needs amending, your time is affected and potentially written off, not the manager's or the partner's time.

In a small practice, you are more likely to be responsible for the preparation of the compliance work. When you are working out a time budget for a job, you need to still take into account the time spent:

- getting the work in from the client / meeting the client;
- logging the work into the practice workflow management system;
- getting the documents ready for the client;
- preparing the invoice;
- attending a client meeting or some form of contact at the end of the job.

Do not make the mistake of just dividing last year's accounting fees by your charge out rate and thinking that is the amount of time you have for the compliance work.

If in doubt, ask your manager to give you a time frame for the work you will be undertaking. Then, if it looks like you cannot complete it in that timeframe, let your manager know as soon as possible. Explain to your manager what you think is the cause of the delay. There are a number of ways the work is different from one year to the next; a change in the software; more transactions; ill-health of business owner making it difficult to obtain information. It is always better to communicate with a client the reason for additional costs this year well before finishing the work.

2. How many weeks do you work per year?

First take out the four weeks annual leave. Then deduct another four weeks for public holidays, personal leave and professional development. That really only leave forty-four weeks on average each year to achieve your goal in fees invoiced.

3. How many hours in your day must be chargeable?

In every day there are times when you are working but not chargeable. Maybe you are locating the client files or relevant information, attending meetings or researching. The number of hours a day that your time is not chargeable is a critical factor in how we manage our billings.

This means that if you fall behind your personal time budget in one month, you have to carefully look at how you are going to make up the time in the next month to get back on track. It is also important to keep in mind how you manage the non-chargeable "re-do work" especially if you are a graduate or trainee accountant. If you are a graduate or trainee then mistakes will happen and work will need to be re-done. The client cannot be charged for this additional time on their file.

Some practices work on billable hours per year so it is really important that either when being interviewed or before you start work, you are aware of what your personal time budget is and the timeframe you are given to achieve it.

If you are interested, you'll do what's convenient. If you are committed, you'll do whatever it takes.
- John Assaraf

4. *Your charge out rate*

Your charge out rate is a combination of both your actual cost to the practice and your skill level. A graduate will not be charged out at the same rate as an intermediate accountant, who in turn, is not charged out at the same rate as a senior accountant.

Do you know what your personal time budget and charge out rate is?

Your charge out rate normally reflects the multiple that your firm is expecting you to achieve.

Assuming you are on a salary package of $60,000. Your personal budget might be to earn three times your salary or $180,000. If your charge out rate is $165 per hour and if you can invoice for twenty-five hours in your working week for forty-four weeks of the year, you will generate just over $180,000 for your firm.

If your employer works on a three times multiple, then if you achieve twenty-five productive invoice hours per week each week you work, you will have met your personal time goal and the minimum requirement of your employer.

So you turn up to work on time, work diligently throughout the day, minimise your time on social media, attend meetings, fit in with the team and average twenty-five chargeable hours per week. Do you think this qualifies you for a pay rise? Actually, all this is just the minimum expectation of any employee.

If you want a pay increase then you must understand the impact that will have on your charge out rate and the minimum expectation of client billings from you.

And if you are not achieving the multiple set by your employer, then you are in serious danger of losing your job. If you have no idea what you bill out or what is expected then you also don't know how close you may be to being unemployed.

When you work in Public Practice, especially in small firms, there is nowhere to hide. You can't sit quietly at your desk and hope that you won't be noticed. In Public Practice, as in any professional position, you are accountable.

It can be at first stressful thinking about these issues of accountability and charge out rates but it also provides a simple and very clear framework for you to work out your "value" to the practice you work in.

5

Managing your Manager

Your employer/manager is human, like you are. They have probably been in your position too. Your employer is running a business and trying to work in it as well. All business owners are concerned about cash flow, preparing for client meetings, answering staff questions, trying to meet their own personal budgets, dealing with admin matters and often all in one day, each and every day.

It is at times very stressful running any business and it is no different for an accounting and tax practice. And managers experience all the normal highs and lows and pressures in their private lives that any staff member experiences.

Here are some hints and tips on how to "manage" your employer/manager to achieve and maintain a productive, two way working relationship.

Asking a technical question

If you need to ask a technical question, do some research first.

Outline the problem or issue and provide any supporting evidence to help explain the situation. Then suggest an answer or solution and the reason why you think it will work. Do not ask for help without researching first and thinking (hard) about a solution. If you don't, how will you learn and improve? The answers are not always handed out in university. As you gain experience and seniority as an accountant you are expected to research and arrive at your own professional conclusions.

Do not under any circumstances walk in with "knock, knock, just a quickie" then proceed to launch into a technical question about a client that you may have just spent hours working on but your manager has no idea about.

Your manager's time is valuable so maximise the useful information and minimise the time that your boss needs to spend trying to understanding the problem.

If you have made a mistake, own it

We all make mistakes. More experienced accountants are more likely to pick up their mistakes before the work is checked, or at least before the work has gone to the client. The less experience the accountant has, the more likely someone else will discover the error.

If, despite our best efforts, a mistake occurs, how do we manage it? If you have made a mistake first own up to it and apologise.

Then, how is it to be corrected? Use that process to understand how it was fixed and make copies or notes so that if the issue occurs again, you have a reference point for assistance.

If you don't own the mistake you are doomed to keep repeating it. Don't make a compounding error in thinking that the person checking your work was just being pedantic. Learn why it was wrong, understand how it was corrected and never make the same mistake again.

Don't lose confidence, learn from your mistakes

No one likes making mistakes and few like having their mistakes found by others, especially when you put a lot into getting the work done and you thought you had done a great job.

While you are learning it is hard not to lose confidence and easy to become disheartened. Talk to you manager and explain how you feel. Don't sulk at your desk or avoid talking to your boss. It will be fairly obvious what is going on so if this is how you feel, you need to decide what sort of person you are:

- are you able to dig deep and persevere and keep getting feedback until the "wins" outnumber the mistakes, or
- are you going to sulk, not admit your role in this process and then look for a job where maybe the work is easier or they have "better training"?

Your manager will be watching to see how you react. Talk to

your boss or someone else in your team. Don't give up unless you are prepared to admit that maybe public accounting may not be for you.

> *One thing is certain in Business. You and everyone around you will make mistakes.*
> *- Richard Branson*

Asking for annual leave

Holidays are important so do not wait until the last minute to ask for time off. As soon as you are planning a holiday talk to your boss.

Most Public Practices will have an internal policy about annual leave so if your request is for time off outside of the practice policy then give as much notice as you can.

Is your manager working long hours?

In a small practice, the long working hours of your manager often means the practice as a whole is underperforming. If the practice owner is so hands on that they are a major producer of the monthly income then it could be a sign that the accountants working in the practice are underperforming.

Every practice owner tries to balance staff capacity with the client base. If a practice is growing fast, then that balance has not been struck so long hours are worked to cope until a solution can be found.

This is a critical time to make sure that you are meeting your productivity and invoicing budget. Don't assume you know what is going on; if you have any questions you must ask.

6

Professional Development

When you complete your degree and graduate do not think that your days of study are behind you. They are really just beginning.

The degree you have completed provides a foundation and base level information. As a subject, accounting offers graduates the choice of learning about industry, government, public practice, auditing or insolvency. Whatever stream of accounting you focus on, additional and ongoing professional development is essential.

Whilst professional development is widely understood to refer to your profession, it also encompasses the "soft" skills we need to learn as well.

It is important that every professional considers what skills need to be maintained and which skills must be developed to advance their career.

Technical Professional Development

There is a lot of content available on the internet. I use the internet when I'm researching static accounting information such as formulas for KPI's. I also use it for researching information on the tax office website. If I need to learn about recent tax law changes I always pay to attend a seminar or webinar or seek advice from another professional.

There are a large number of organisations that offer technical tax and accounting updates, in particular the various accounting bodies amongst others.

If you are a member of a professional organisation you will be required to complete a minimum number of professional development hours. Attending a day seminar and attending a monthly discussion group will not only give you the required hours, but more importantly maintain your technical knowledge and build long term relationships with other professionals.

Check with your employer as they may have a preferred provider of professional development and ask about what sort of professional development they think would benefit you most.

There are a number of options for accessing professional development sessions. The use of technology means that you can attend either an external session or a webinar.

Webinars tend to be sixty to ninety minutes long and often

notes are delivered electronically the same day. Most webinars are available for a period of time as they are recorded. Listening to a webinar is a productive way to use a lunch break.

It is also an opportunity for the more experienced team members to sit in with the less experienced accountants and use the webinar topic as a discussion point for internal training.

> *Without continuous personal development, you are now all that you will ever become.*
> *- Eli Cohen*

If your employer pays for you to attend a session or you attend during work hours, then:

- Make sure you attend all of it, unless given prior permission to leave early;
- Arrive on time;
- Be prepared to give a short briefing of the day to the other members of your team. This is a great way to embed the learning, learn to speak publicly (which we all have to do at some time), and to share knowledge within the team.

Non Technical Professional Development

There is an equally important type of development you need to consider – personal development. Often referred to as "soft skills" the investment you make in yourself for personal development rounds you out as a professional.

No one comes out of university with all the life and technical skills they will ever need during their professional career. Everyone can benefit from personal development in areas such as:

- Public speaking;
- Working in a team;
- Time management;
- How to manage clients;
- How to manage co-workers;
- How to manage conflict;
- How to write effective letters or emails;
- Marketing and publicity techniques;
- How to run a successful meeting.

You may be naturally quiet or shy or you may be outgoing and gregarious. Everyone can benefit from attending sessions on communicating more effectively and working with different personalities, which ultimately, all these soft skills are about.

You can be a great technician but if you can not communicate effectively, then your career may be limited or not a fulfilling as it would otherwise be. You will have limited time in front of clients and ultimately, that means a limited career.

Learning how to write or speak about a technical issue in a non-technical way is essential when you are communicating directly with a client. It is also important if you are training staff.

7

How to integrate clients into the practice

There is no better way to get know a client than to be involved in the process of their integration or onboarding into the practice.

Do not make the mistake of dismissing this as merely "admin" work. If you don't involve yourself in this process, the admin staff may have a better relationship with the client than you.

Think about it from the client's perspective. While they may be sure about the decision to leave their previous accountant, they are hoping they have made the right decision to come to your firm. In these early "honeymoon" stages of the client relationship there is usually a lot of goodwill, but this can easily be destroyed.

Use this time to get to know your client. Don't be afraid to ask questions. Check with the person who handled the initial call or email if it was not you.

Client Integration - Technical

There can be a lot of databases to update when you take over a client. If you do not update each of them yourself, at least check to see that every address, phone number and name is correct. Specifically, check every database that will be used to generate client work.

The most common databases:

Australian Securities and Investment Commission (ASIC).

If there is a company involved it is vital that you check the following information is correct:

- Registered Office – should be either be the client's home or business address or the accounting firm;
- Directors – check that their home addresses are correctly recorded and that their dates of birth are correct;
- Shareholders – check that their home addresses are correctly recorded;
- Business Office – this should be the work place of the client;
- Log into ASIC and run a Debtor's report on the client to see if they owe any ASIC fees. If the addresses have not been correctly maintained it is possible that the Annual Return has not been properly completed or lodged. The ASIC Debtor's report will

tell you if there are any serious issues facing the client that they may be unaware of;

- Make sure that the Directors and Shareholders listed on ASIC are the people / entities you expected to see.

The Australian Tax Office (ATO) Tax Agent Portal (TAP)

The Tax Agent Portal is one of the most used databases in a practice. If you have not already done so, spend some time looking at each function in the navigator bar and the information that is available about the client.

Check that the addresses of the client are correct, both for mailing and home addresses. Have the tax agent details been updated correctly? What tax type registrations are in place for the client? For instance, is the client registered for GST?

> *Success consists of going from failure to failure without loss of enthusiasm.*
> *- Winston Churchill*

Progressively, the ATO is moving towards electronic communications as their preference. There are a number of forms and applications for both the client and the practice that can be accessed from the TAP. Make sure you know where to find these forms and how to follow up the ATO communication.

Workers Compensation Insurance

Each state has a different Workers Compensation Insurance

scheme. If the client has employees, obtain the user name and log in details to help validate the Statement of Annual Remuneration. Even if the client self lodges, it is important to verify that the correct figures were lodged.

State Payroll Tax.

As with Workers Compensation Insurance schemes in your state, obtain the user name and log in details to assist in validating the information lodged by the client.

Client Integration – Non technical

Clients are generally very tolerant and it takes a lot of mistakes or poor service for them to change accounting firms, especially if they have been a client of the firm for a long time. When you have an opportunity to meet with a potential client, take the time to understand why they are changing and what level of service they would like.

During the initial meeting with a client, they are assessing you and the practice, but you are also assessing the client. The questions you need to consider are:

- Are you able to manage this client and their tax and accounting requirements?
- Is this client going to need professional services or skills that you do not have?

- Are you confident that you can meet the client expectations of service and support?
- Are there any conflicts of interest or ethical reasons why this appointment should not be accepted?

There are various reasons why clients change accountants: the fees are too high; the service is poor; they are passed down a chain from one accountant to the next; their emails are not answered and calls not returned. But in the end I think it all comes down to the client not feeling valued.

There is no definitive list of questions to ask but start by getting to know the client's background. Then move into business issues being faced at present, then wealth creation and finally succession if they're running a business.

Do not worry if you don't feel comfortable asking a specific question – in this initial meeting you are trying to get the client to open up as much as possible about themselves and their business.

- How long have they been in business?
- Are they happy with how their business is operating at the moment?
- Is there a business issue really worrying them at the moment?
- How are they financially?
  - Do they own their home?
  - Do they have superannuation?

- ° Have they investments outside of super?
- ° What debt do they have?
- ° For what business plans do they need funding?
- ° Do they understand their current business structure and financial situation?
- ° Do they have any questions about how they are structured at the moment?
- ° How long do they intend to work?
- ° Do they have someone in the family or in the business who will be able to take it over?
- ° What was the reason they went into business originally? Has that goal been achieved?
- ° What keeps them awake at night?

Document their responses. Keep a file note and even think about drafting an email to follow up on the meeting notes, restating what you have understood, what you have to do following the meeting and what you would like the client to do.

Make it easy for the client to understand what to do to become your client. What processes or forms need to be completed in order to properly integrate the client? Do you have all the information needed from the client?

8

The future of Public Accounting

The introduction of GST and the development of the world wide web had a significant impact on public accounting. Those changes are now completely adopted by small business owners.

Business clients either had to learn basic bookkeeping or engage a bookkeeper to help them comply with the GST lodgement requirements. As a result, there has been a huge increase in the number of bookkeepers and now they can register to lodge a tax form by becoming a BAS agent with the Australian Tax Office.

The internet has not only enabled small business to reach out and sell worldwide but it has also enabled access the world wide business support community.

Online programs enable the bookkeeping to be done on any device, anywhere. This means that any small business owner can outsource bookkeeping support from anywhere in the world, often at a lower hourly rate than can be sourced locally.

When the bookwork is up to date, the accounting compliance also can be outsourced. Again, at a much cheaper rate than can be sourced locally.

Once the compliance has been managed, there are any number of business advisory services that can be outsourced. It is in business advisory services that I see the best opportunities available for the public accounting profession in Australia.

Think about a small business that you know. The typical list of service providers would be:

- Accountants
- Bookkeepers
- Insurance
- Legal advice
- Finance Broking
- Human Resources / Payroll
- Marketing
- Financial Planning

Which of these services cannot be better handled online or over the phone? Every small business owner now has the opportunity to work with a service provider that may not even be in the same state or country as they are.

I believe the role of the Public Accountant has to be focused more on being a business advisor than on handling compliance work. It's still important to get the compliance work done as accurately and efficiently as possible. You can only advise on a business when you know the Profit and Loss and Balance Sheet are complete and correct. Managing the compliance work must be seen as the first step in supporting your clients.

Moving into a business advisory role can be daunting but the same tools are available to you as they are to the rest of the world. The world wide web has a lot of information so make some time and start researching.

The availability of online bookkeeping programs also offers an opportunity to provide additional services to a client. Most of the online bookkeeping options available to small businesses can produce management reports based on real time current data. There is also a growing number of other software programs and apps that manage a specific task or event and that link directly into bookkeeping software.

Sad fact: generally, clients don't value compliance work. At all. It is a financial burden and a yearly regulatory event that has to happen to avoid fines and penalties. And at the end there is usually a tax bill. So there is little joy in it for the client., and by this stage the information is so far out of date that it is of little further value.

No matter how long they have been a client, if someone comes along offering a cheaper service, easier to access and nothing less than they are getting now from you then why wouldn't the client move? If you are only offering compliance support then be prepared to see a big change in your client base in the next few years.

Business clients need a partner. Someone they not only trust but who can help find the answers to the problems they face. You don't need to know the answer to everything off the top of your head. No one can do that. But, you can help in a number of other ways.

> *The greatest danger in times of turbulence is not the turbulence – it is to act with yesterday's logic.*
> *- Peter Drucker*

Once the compliance work is complete, look at the figures and tell your clients what they reveal to you. Some areas to consider would be:

Profit:

Has the business made any money? Is that Profit consistent over the last 5 years? What is the Profit as a percentage of Turnover?

Sales:

Were the sales this year higher than last year? What is the Sales trend over the last 5 years? If it is decreasing is the business viable in the short term? If the sales are increasing is this putting pressure on cash flow?

Balance Sheet:

Are true Current Assets more than true Current Liabilities? Is there too much money tied up in stock or debtors? Are the Net Assets growing or decreasing? When I say 'true' I mean net of any money owing to or by family that is unlikely to be repaid quickly.

If your client has a trading business, do they know how to work out the cost of a product or service, remembering to take overheads into account? Do they understand that buying stock is not an expense in the Profit and Loss but an Asset in the Balance Sheet?

There are lots of ways to review the figures and help your client understand what their financial story is. Ask you clients what worries them or keeps them awake at night. Once you've got an answer or an idea on what their concerns are, look to the figures. What information is sitting there right in front of you waiting to be used in the telling of their financial story?

Business owners need our help. Too often, the help they go looking for is offered by business coaches. Have a look online and search for a "business coach" and see how many alternatives there are. Then search for training or courses on how to be a business coach.

I think the growing influence of business coaches reflects that business owners are in need of "business partners" and too often the accounting profession is absent in this space. If your client has a relationship with a business coach, then like any other professional relationship, define your roles and work together.

Also, the robots are coming and this will also have an impact on our service delivery model. Like outsourcing or online programs, the potential of artificial intelligence will take a while to be fully realised. But whether a robot processed the client data or a human did, it is the interpretation of the data and the conclusions drawn from it that matters to the client.

When GST began there was a lot of talk about the impact of accountants losing work and the cost of the extra compliance to the client. There was a lot of fear at the time that "compliance was dead". This hasn't turned out to the be true. What is true, though, is that tax law and technology changes constantly. As a profession, we need to adapt to survive.

Whilst there are so many new bookkeeping programs on the market, the same old adage applies to when clients prepared ledger books and journals: the final result depends on the quality of the work going in. Computer programs, in themselves are no guarantee of quality data entry.

This is where I see the role of the public accountant in future. We need to work closely with bookkeepers to ensure we don't inherit a "computerised shoebox", full of scraps of random data.

We can work closely with financial planners, finance brokers, business coaches and lawyers as we try to protect our client's assets or grow their wealth or protect their family.

As accountants, we are best placed to help our clients understand their businesses better and set meaningful financial goals and targets that we can then monitor through a regular review of their data. Remember, every three months a client's work is updated if they need to lodge a BAS. There is always something valuable to talk to a client about.

A short note on becoming a tax agent. Whilst not for everyone, for a lot of accountants who work in tax the natural progression is to apply for a Tax Agent registration.

There is a misconception that by processing enough tax returns and financial statements that you can apply for a tax agent registration. Becoming a tax agent is akin to completing an apprenticeship. Processing the work isn't enough on its own. Are you personally able to:

- Complete the client's work;
- resolve any tax issues;
- communicate directly with clients;
- answer queries and ensure that the client understands the complexities of the issue.

When there is a mistake, as sometimes there are, do you contact the client, explain the situation, and take the heat and manage the fallout by rebuilding the client relationship and their confidence in you and the work undertaken for them? Or do you pass it onto your manager or partner?

Have you ever said 'No" to a client who was insistent about a tax claim or document to be signed that you knew to be wrong? Tax laws are a complex area and the laws are often changing.

If you think it is stressful when you are an employee it is more stressful if you are in business and relying on the income from that client. Not wanting to lose a client can be a powerful motivator. It may lead you into doing something that you wouldn't normally do or that you know you shouldn't do.

Get as much exposure to client matters as you can so that when you do apply for your registration as a tax agent you are well prepared.

You are putting your assets and your livelihood at risk once you start lodging returns. Don't aim for the minimum experience and then apply. Be as prepared as you can be.

9

Conclusion

Public Practice is extremely rewarding, but it isn't for everyone. Many accountants come into public accounting and find the complexities of learning our tax system overwhelming. For others it is the burden of responsibility that is difficult.

Personally, I love the variety of work and that I can help people. After all these years, I still struggle with the pace of change and with client expectations. What profession doesn't have its challenges?

One thing I've learned over the years is that every industry, every job undergoes change. Change happens frequently but rarely without warning. All industries go through their own cycle of change and disruption. What are you going to do to give yourself the best chance of not just having a job but having an ongoing career?

Completing a degree in accounting doesn't make you professional. The degree is the first step in an ongoing journey of continuing education and professional development. Don't be passive about your continuing education. Your employer will provide some technical training and updates but there is much that you can do yourself.

With so much information available on the web there is an opportunity to thoroughly explore areas that interest you. Take advantage of the internet library and invest in not only the technical aspects of your work but also in the soft skills that will round you off as a professional accountant.

Join a discussion group and develop a network of accountants and related professionals.

> *Change is the law of life and those who look only to the past or present are certain to miss the future.*
> *- John F. Kennedy*

Whether you are planning to go out on your own or operate as a partner, you need to work on attracting and then managing clients.

As a tax agent in public practice you can really be in control of your destiny.

Linda McGowan

After graduating with a Bachelor of Business (Accounting), Linda McGowan spent four years in corporate roles before moving into public practice. She worked in a small team reporting to the two partners as she honed her tax and small business accounting skills at a time when the use of computers in public practice was still novel. Opportunities for professional development seemed very limited until one of the partners suggested Linda join a CPA Discussion Group. This turned out to be fantastic advice and the peers she met in that group have provided support and friendship for decades. Linda has been running her own practice since 1992. This book distils the public practice fundamentals she believes every public accountant needs to know.